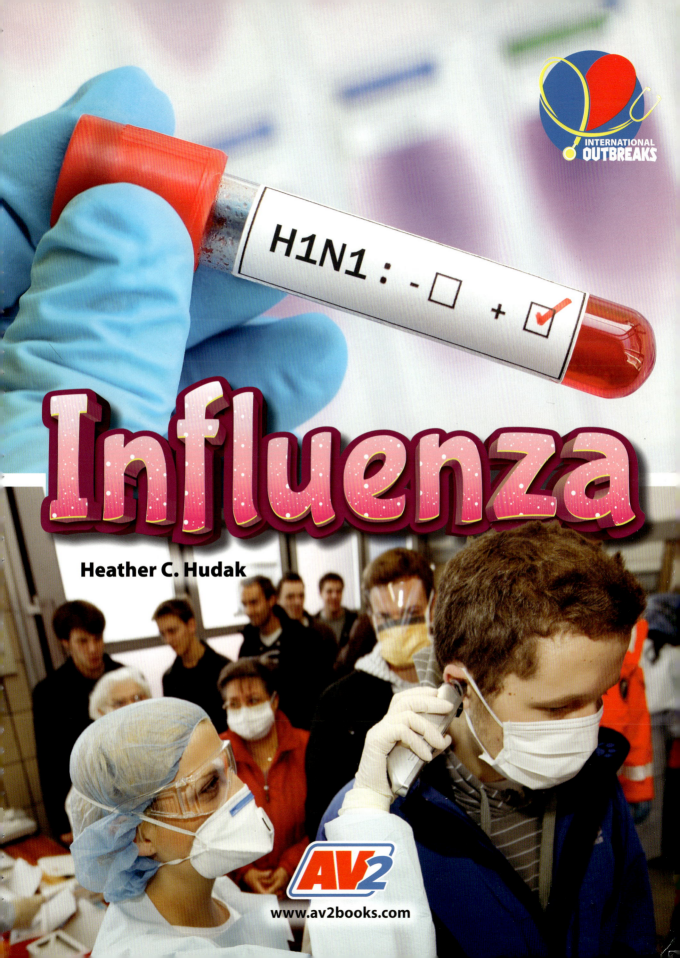

Step 1
Go to www.av2books.com

Step 2
Enter this unique code

UWEQZGNXF

Step 3
Explore your interactive eBook!

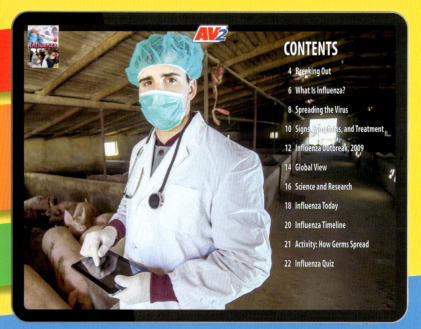

CONTENTS
- 4 Breaking Out
- 6 What Is Influenza?
- 8 Spreading the Virus
- 10 Signs, Symptoms, and Treatment
- 12 Influenza Outbreak, 2009
- 14 Global View
- 16 Science and Research
- 18 Influenza Today
- 20 Influenza Timeline
- 21 Activity: How Germs Spread
- 22 Influenza Quiz

AV2 is optimized for use on any device

Your interactive eBook comes with...

Contents
Browse a live contents page to easily navigate through resources

Audio
Listen to sections of the book read aloud

Videos
Watch informative video clips

Weblinks
Gain additional information for research

Try This!
Complete activities and hands-on experiments

Key Words
Study vocabulary, and complete a matching word activity

Quizzes
Test your knowledge

Slideshows
View images and captions

... and much, much more!

View new titles and product videos at www.av2books.com

Influenza

CONTENTS

Breaking Out 4
What Is Influenza? 6
Spreading the Virus 8
Signs, Symptoms, and Treatment 10
Influenza Outbreak, 2009 12
Global View 14
Science and Research 16
Influenza Today 18
Influenza Timeline 20
Activity: How Germs Spread 21
Influenza Quiz 22
Key Words/Index 23

✺ Influenza is a disease that can cause fever, cough, aches and pains, and a runny nose.

Breaking Out

Diseases happen all over the world. They can happen anywhere and at any time. Scientists study the different diseases. They try to find out what causes each disease and learn about its signs and symptoms. Scientists work to stop diseases from **infecting** people. One of the ways they do this is by keeping track of how many people get the same disease at the same time and place each year. This lets them estimate how many people they think will get the disease in the future.

Sometimes, the number of people who get a disease is higher than scientists expect. This is called an outbreak. It happens when there is a sudden rise in the number of cases of the disease. An outbreak can last days, weeks, months, or even years. It can take place in one community or across many countries. An epidemic happens when a disease is not well **contained**.

FAST FACT

Sometimes, a disease is so deadly that any cases at all are a big problem. Other times, the disease is very rare. Scientists do not expect to see any cases of it, so just a few cases can be an outbreak. Scientists may also be surprised when a new disease appears. This is what happened with H1N1 in 2009.

Influenza 5

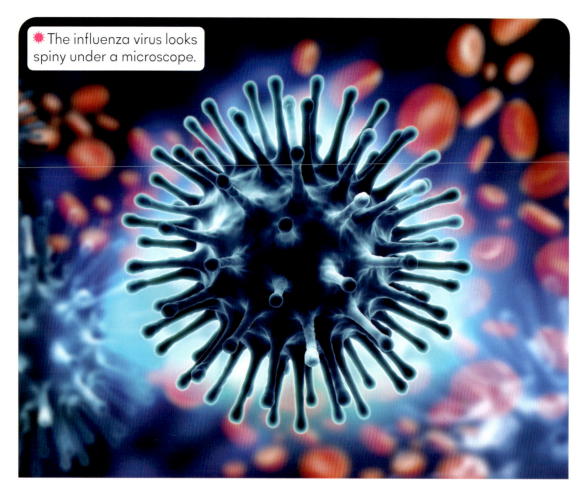

★ The influenza virus looks spiny under a microscope.

What Is Influenza?

Influenza is also called the flu. It is a common **respiratory illness** that attacks a person's throat, nose, and lungs. The flu **virus** infects people all over the world. It is very common. Anyone can get it. People are more likely to get it during flu season, which often takes place in fall and winter. December through February is the most common time to catch the flu.

Flu pandemics have taken place for centuries. One of the first known flu pandemics took place in 1580. The virus spread from Asia to Africa in the summer months. It then spread to Europe and the Americas. More than 8,000 people died in Rome, Italy.

Flu Facts

About **3,000 droplets** come out of the nose when a person sneezes.

Sneeze droplets travel at about **100 miles per hour** (161 kilometers per hour).

Flu viruses can live on objects for **several hours**.

About **20 to 30 percent** of people who have the flu virus show no symptoms.

Influenza

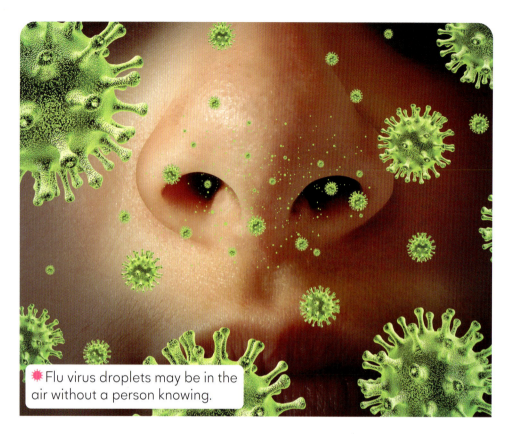

🌟 Flu virus droplets may be in the air without a person knowing.

Spreading the Virus

The flu virus is very **contagious**. It spreads from person to person. Tiny droplets come out of the nose and mouth when a sick person sneezes. People nearby breathe in these droplets. The flu spreads very quickly in crowded places. People should avoid places where others gather if they feel sick. Schools, offices, and concert halls are a few examples of places to avoid.

The flu can also spread through contact with infected objects. Sometimes, people cough or sneeze into their hands. Then, they touch an object such as a doorknob or cell phone before they wash their hands. The object gets infected droplets on it. People who touch the object may then get the virus if they touch their nose, eyes, or mouth without washing their hands first.

* When people sneeze into their hands, they spread germs to anything that they touch.

Animal Infections

Sometimes, flu viruses can spread from animals to humans. Birds and pigs are known to carry flu viruses, for instance. Humans can get the virus by touching an infected animal. Sometimes, people get viruses when they eat meat from an infected animal. Fortunately, this does not happen often. It is not easy for an animal virus to jump to a human.

*Throat swabs can be used to test for the flu.

Signs, Symptoms, and Treatment

People infected with the flu often have a fever and chills. They may feel weak and tired. Sometimes, their muscles ache. They may also have head and stomach pain. A sore throat, cough, and runny or stuffy nose are other signs of the flu. People who have the flu can spread their germs one or two days before they show any signs. They can keep spreading the virus for five to seven days after they first feel sick.

Most people get better on their own after about a week. All they need to do is drink plenty of fluids and get enough rest. They can also take medicines to help with their symptoms. Some people become very sick with the flu. They may even get pneumonia. This can be deadly. These people could need help from a doctor. Doctors may prescribe **antiviral** drugs to treat the flu.

Cold or Flu?

Many people think the flu is the same as the common cold. The diseases have some of the same symptoms. However, they are caused by different types of viruses. Colds form slowly. The flu comes on fast and without warning. It is often much worse than a cold.

SYMPTOMS	COLD	FLU
Fever	Rare	High, can last for 3 to 4 days
Headache	Rare	Common
Aches	Slight	Common, can be severe
Fatigue, weakness	Mild	Intense, can last a few weeks
Stuffy or runny nose	Common	Sometimes
Sneezing	Usual	Sometimes
Sore throat	Common	Sometimes
Cough	Mild to moderate	Common, can become severe

Influenza

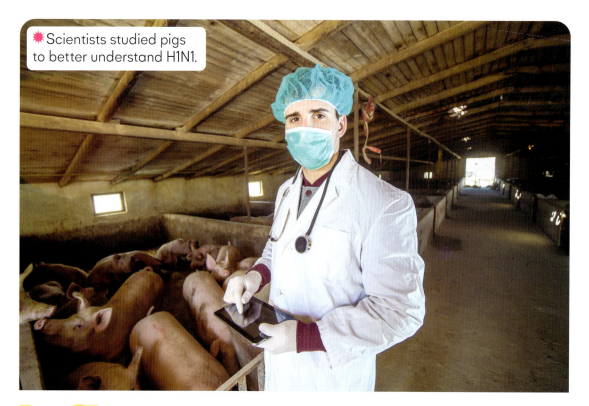

*Scientists studied pigs to better understand H1N1.

Influenza Outbreak, 2009

In the spring of 2009, a new flu virus was discovered. It was a type of H1N1 virus. The virus was first spotted in the United States. Two children in different parts of California caught the flu at about the same time. They had never met. It was not likely that one of the children had given the virus to the other child.

This was cause for concern. The H1N1 virus was similar to other flu viruses, but people did not have any immunity to it because it was new. It was also more contagious than other flu viruses. More people became sick as a result. Scientists wondered where the virus came from and how it spread. They began to study it more closely. It took time to learn the facts. Scientists found that the H1N1 flu was likely a mix of a bird, pig, and human flu.

H1N1 around the World by August 2009

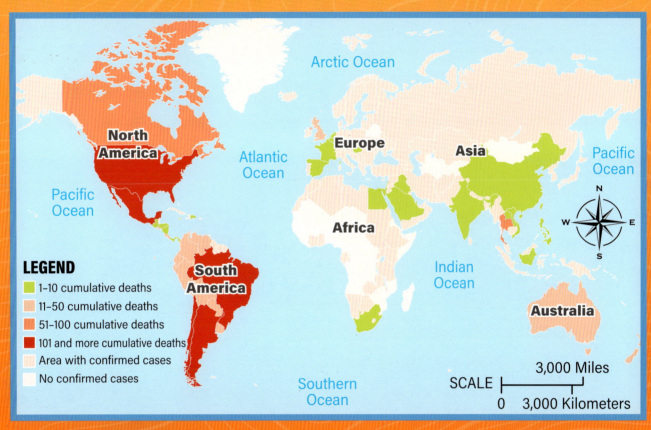

Scientists think that H1N1 **first infected swine**, or **pigs**, in Mexico.

The H1N1 virus then **jumped from pigs to humans**. This is how it got the nickname "swine flu."

H1N1 **quickly spread** across the **Americas**.

Influenza

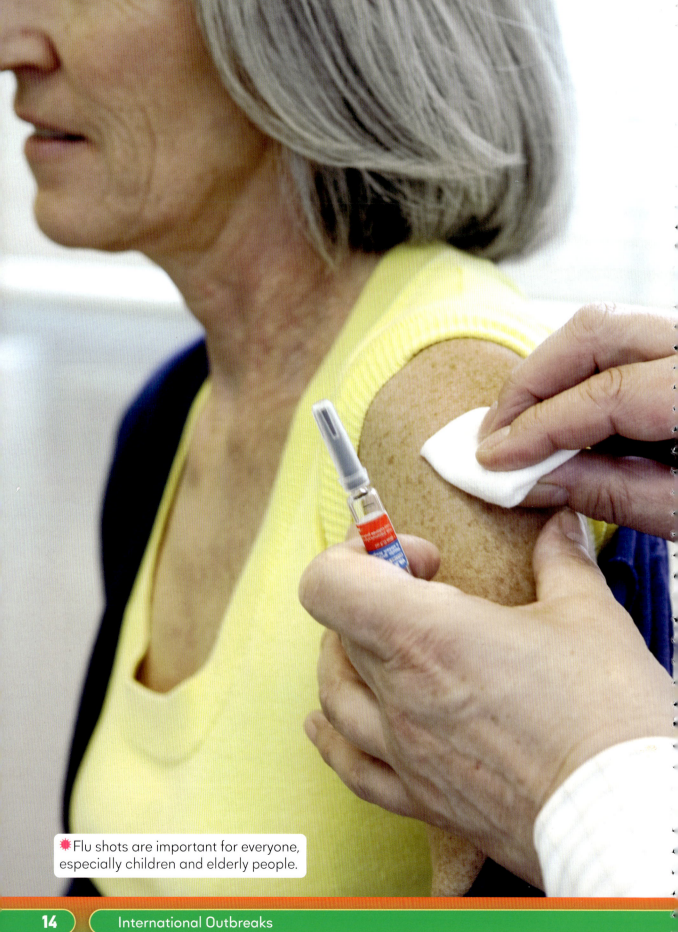

✹ Flu shots are important for everyone, especially children and elderly people.

Global View

It was not long before H1N1 made its way to other parts of the world. People who had traveled by airplane from infected parts of Mexico carried the virus home with them. Soon, H1N1 was in Spain, Germany, the United Kingdom, Canada, New Zealand, Austria, and Israel, among other countries. On June 11, 2009, the **World Health Organization** (WHO) declared H1N1 a pandemic. It was the first flu pandemic in 40 years.

Scientists worked hard to make a **vaccine**. The first doses were given out in October. Finally, the spread of the virus began to slow down. WHO declared the pandemic over on August 11, 2010. Experts believe the virus killed as many as 575,400 people around the world.

Just the Facts

Information is everywhere. Not all of it is true. Sometimes, people share their thoughts and opinions about an issue, such as H1N1. They may not know all the facts. It is important to listen to what experts have to say. Scientists, health workers, and government websites are some of the best sources for facts on viruses.

Science and Research

Influenza is very common. There are **seasonal** flu outbreaks each year. Today, H1N1 is one of the common flu viruses that strike each year. Scientists are always looking for new ways to treat flu viruses. Each year, they try to guess which flu viruses will be most common. They choose three or four strains and then make a vaccine for them.

Vaccines are the best way for people to protect themselves from the flu. They help people build immunity against a virus. People are less at risk of getting the virus at all with vaccines, and their symptoms will likely be milder if they do get the flu. Doctors recommend that people over six months of age get the flu vaccine before the start of flu season each year.

FAST FACT

Children under the age of 18 are more than twice as likely to get the flu as adults over age 65.

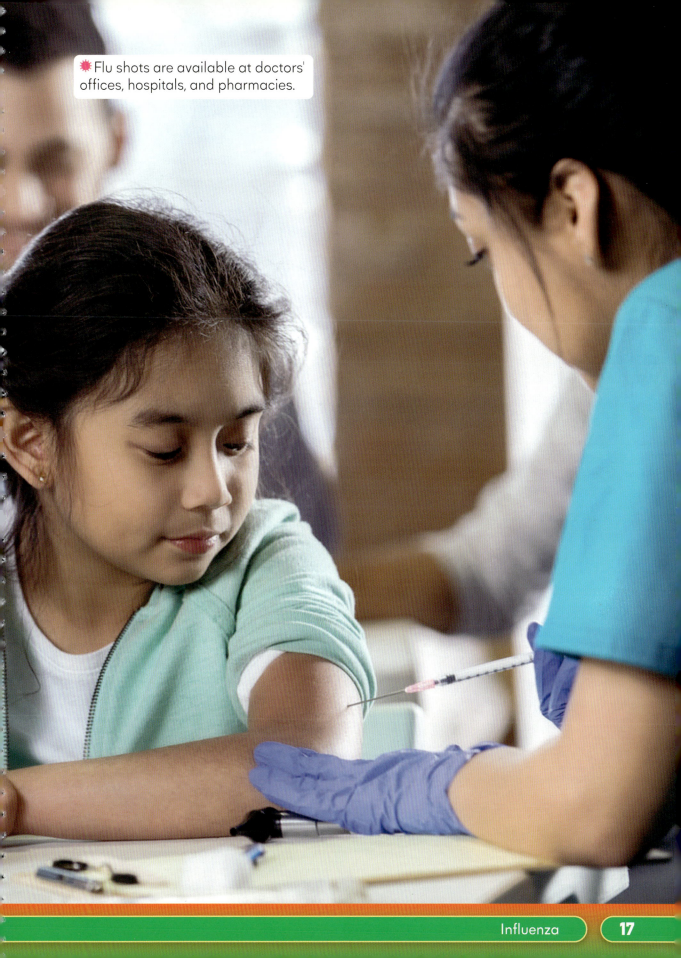

✺ Flu shots are available at doctors' offices, hospitals, and pharmacies.

Influenza

✹ Each year, about 31 million Americans see their doctor for the flu.

Influenza Today

The number of people who get the flu varies from year to year. There are as many as 1 billion cases of the flu around the world in any given year. Of these cases, roughly 3 to 5 million are severe, and about 290,000 to 650,000 people die. The flu infects between 5 and 15 percent of the U.S. population. There are about 9 to 49 million flu cases each year in the United States alone.

Children aged six months to five years, pregnant women, people with ongoing health issues, and adults over age 65 are more likely to have severe flu symptoms. Most people recover from the flu. Even people with very bad symptoms get better with proper rest and care. Deaths from the flu are rare for most people. Only major outbreaks, epidemics, and pandemics are causes for concern.

Peak Month of Flu Activity, 1982–2018

✸ Flu droplets spread easily when someone who is infected sneezes or coughs.

Influenza   19

Influenza Timeline

1580
The earliest known flu pandemic takes place around the world. Thousands of people die from the virus.

1918
An H1N1 flu virus known as the Spanish flu infects about one-third of the world's population. More than 50 million people die.

1957–1958
H2N2, or the Asian flu, kills about 1.1 million people worldwide.

1968–1969
Approximately 1 million people around the world die during the Hong Kong flu pandemic.

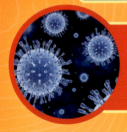

2009
More than 60 million people contract a new H1N1 virus.

2019–2020
The 2019–2020 flu season starts out as one of the highest on record, but gets eclipsed by the COVID-19 pandemic.

ACTIVITY
How Germs Spread

Viruses are very tiny germs that are all around us. They are so small that people need a special microscope to see them. Germs can spread quickly from person to person. Try this activity to see how fast germs can spread. It also shows why you need to wash your hands well to get rid of germs.

What You Need

- Glitter
- Hand lotion
- Bucket
- Soap
- Water
- Paper towels

What to Do

1. Put a drop of lotion on your hands. Rub your hands together to spread the lotion around.
2. Hold your hands over the bucket. Put a pinch of glitter into the palm of one hand. Imagine the glitter is a flu virus.
3. Make a fist with the hand that has the glitter. Then, open your hand and spread out your fingers. Did the glitter spread to the rest of your hand?
4. Rub your hands together and then touch another person's hands or some objects in the room. Did the glitter spread?
5. Now, try wiping the glitter off with a paper towel. Did all the glitter come off?
6. Next, use the soap and water to wash your hands. Be sure to wash the tops of your fingers and thumbs. Wash between each finger, too. Handwashing should take about 20 seconds. You can sing the birthday song twice to make sure you wash long enough.
7. Use a clean paper towel to dry your hands well. Did all the glitter come off?

Influenza

INFLUENZA QUIZ

1 What is another name for influenza?

2 When was the earliest known flu pandemic?

3 What are common flu symptoms?

4 Where can people go to get flu shots?

5 Who can get influenza?

6 How does influenza spread?

7 What was the name of the 2009 flu pandemic?

8 What might doctors prescribe to treat the flu?

ANSWERS
1. The flu
2. 1580
3. Fever, chills, feeling weak and tired, achy muscles, head and stomach pain, sore throat, cough, and runny or stuffy nose
4. Doctors' offices, hospitals, and pharmacies
5. Anyone
6. Through infected droplets
7. H1N1, or swine flu
8. Antiviral drugs and medicines

22 International Outbreaks

Key Words

antiviral: drugs that fight viruses inside the body

contagious: moves easily from one person to another

contained: kept under control

diseases: illnesses that have certain signs and symptoms

infecting: contaminating a person or object with a disease-causing germ

respiratory illness: a disease that affects the lungs

seasonal: happening at a certain time of year

vaccine: a substance made from a small amount of a disease-causing germ to help provide immunity against that germ

virus: a very small germ that gets inside the body and spreads

World Health Organization: an organization that sets health standards and guidelines that many countries follow

Index

animal 9, 12

cold 11

doctor 10, 12, 16, 17, 18, 22

flu season 6, 16, 19, 20

H1N1 5, 12, 13, 15, 16, 20, 22

Mexico 13, 15

outbreak 5, 16, 18, 20

scientists 5, 12, 13, 15, 16

Spanish flu 20

symptoms 5, 7, 10, 11, 16, 18, 22

vaccine 15, 16

World Health Organization (WHO) 15

Influenza 23

Get the best of both worlds.

AV2 bridges the gap between print and digital.

The expandable resources toolbar enables quick access to content including **videos**, **audio**, **activities**, **weblinks**, **slideshows**, **quizzes**, and **key words**.

Animated videos make static images come alive.

Resource icons on each page help readers to further **explore key concepts**.

Published by AV2
14 Penn Plaza, 9th Floor
New York, NY 10122
Website: www.av2books.com

Copyright ©2021 AV2
All rights reserved. No part of this publication may be reproduced, stored in a retrieval system, or transmitted in any form or by any means, electronic, mechanical, photocopying, recording, or otherwise, without the prior written permission of the publisher.

Library of Congress Control Number: 2020943905

ISBN 978-1-7911-3234-7 (hardcover)
ISBN 978-1-7911-3235-4 (softcover)
ISBN 978-1-7911-3236-1 (multi-user eBook)
ISBN 978-1-7911-3237-8 (single-user eBook)

Printed in Guangzhou, China
1 2 3 4 5 6 7 8 9 0   24 23 22 21 20

082020
101119

Art Director: Terry Paulhus Project Coordinator: Priyanka Das

Every reasonable effort has been made to trace ownership and to obtain permission to reprint copyright material. The publisher would be pleased to have any errors or omissions brought to its attention so that they may be corrected in subsequent printings.

The publisher acknowledges Alamy, Getty Images, iStock, and Shutterstock as its primary image suppliers for this title.